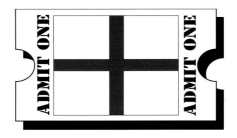

The Huge Clock Named "Big Ben" At The Houses Of Parliament In London

FACES
AND
PLACES

ENGLAND

BY ELMA SCHEMENAUER

THE CHILD'S WORLD® INC.

GRAPHIC DESIGN AND PRODUCTION
Robert E. Bonaker / Graphic Design & Consulting Co.

PHOTO RESEARCH
James R. Rothaus / James R. Rothaus & Associates

COVER PHOTO
English students in uniform
©Bob Krist/CORBIS

Library of Congress Cataloging-in-Publication Data
Schemenauer, Elma.
England / by Elma Schemenauer.
p. cm.
Includes index.
Summary: Briefly surveys the history, geography, plants and
animals, people, and culture of England.
ISBN 1-56766-735-X (lib. reinforced : alk. paper)

1. England — Juvenile literature. [1. England.] I. Title.

DA27.5 .S34 2000
942 — dc21

99-048444

Table
of
Contents

ADMIT ONE

ADMIT ONE

What hat if you were in a spacecraft high above Earth? You would see huge land areas with water around them. These land areas are called **continents**. Some continents are made up of several countries. Though England is on an island, it is part of the continent of Europe.

Western Hemisphere

Eastern Hemisphere

England (white) Is In Both Hemispheres. U.S.A. (green) Is In The West

England, Scotland, and Wales make up the island of *Great Britain*. Along with nearby Northern Ireland, they make up the **United Kingdom**. Waters around England include the Irish Sea and the North Sea. A narrow strip of water, the *English Channel*, separates England from France.

Arctic Ocean

NORTH AMERICA

United States of America

Atlantic Ocean

Pacific Ocean

SOUTH AMERICA

ANTARCTICA

England

EUROPE

ASIA

AFRICA

Indian Ocean

Pacific Ocean

AUSTRALIA

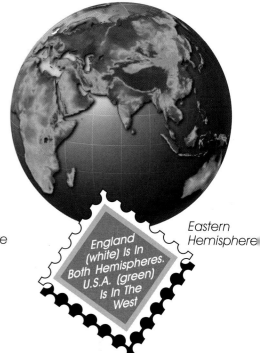

The World Shown Flat

Atlantic
Ocean

NORWAY

SCOTLAND

North Sea

NORTHERN
IRELAND

IRELAND

ENGLAND

WALES

NETHERLANDS

Strait of Dover

GERMANY

English Channel

BELGIUM

FRANCE

Close-Up
of
England

The Cheviot Hills
In Northern England

CHEVIOT HILLS

Lake District

★ London

©WildCountry/CORBIS

The Land

England is shaped like a tall, knobby triangle. In the north are rugged uplands and mountains. In the middle and southeast are low-lying plains and gentle hills. These are home to most of England's big cities. In the southwest are rugged uplands and **moors**. These are lonely, open grasslands. In the southwest are low **plateaus** with highlands rising above them. Several of the highlands are made of granite. Near the coast, the plateaus end in cliffs.

England is as far north as Newfoundland, Canada, but it enjoys warmer winters. In fact, England is so mild that daffodils bloom in February. The country is warmed by the *Gulf Stream*, an ocean current from the sunny south.

Cliffs On The Southern Coast Of England

©Adam Woolfitt/CORBIS

The Cubrian Mountains In The Lake District

©Adam Woolfitt/CORBIS

A Mute Swan On The Lune River Near Lancaster

©Jon Sparks/CORBIS

Trees such as elms, oaks, and beeches once covered much of England. People cleared many trees for farming, but some forests still exist. These include newly planted trees such as pines and spruces. Grasses and low shrubs such as heather grow on England's windswept moors.

A Group Of Deer In Bushey Park Near Hampton

©Patrick Ward/CORBIS

Wild ponies trot over the moors. Among England's other wild animals are hedgehogs, weasels, deer, and red foxes. Otters play in some of the rivers, and seals swim along the seacoasts. Fish include sole, haddock, and herring. Among the country's many birds are swans, wrens, pippits, and blackbirds.

Lancaster

• Hampton

Devon
Moors

©Andrew Brown/Ecoscene/CORBIS

Heather
Growing On A Hill
In The Devon
Moors

Vindolanda
Fort Near
Bardon Mill
Was Built By
Romans

• Bardon Mill

★ London

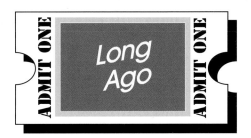

Queen Elizabeth I Was The Founder Of England's Current Government

Among early people in what is now England were hunters, farmers, stoneworkers, and tin miners. About 2,600 years ago, iron-working *Celts* (KELTS) from northern Europe came and set up a kingdom there. A few hundred years later, road-building *Romans* took over. Then came German-speaking *Angles* and *Saxons,* followed by seagoing Vikings.

The last to invade England were French-speaking *Normans,* in the year 1066. Their leader became William I, king of England.

Many kings and queens followed William. In the 1500s, during Queen Elizabeth I's reign, the English claimed Newfoundland (Canada). They also tried to start a **colony** on Roanoke Island (eastern United States).

From then on, they roamed the seas, starting colonies around the world, building an empire.

As this great empire spread, so did the English language and English ideas about fairness in government. After 1707, when England, Scotland, and Wales joined to form Great Britain, this empire became the **British Empire.**

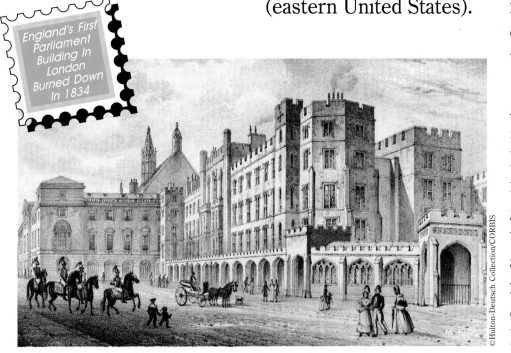

England's First Parliament Building In London Burned Down In 1834

©Francis G. Mayer/CORBIS

©Hulton-Deutsch Collection/CORBIS

England Today

Today England is the most powerful country in the United Kingdom. With the years, ties between the four "mother countries" and the colonies of the former empire have slowly loosened. Most of the former colonies are still friends with the United Kingdom.

Prime Minister Tony Blair In London

©Peter Turnley/CORBIS

However, the United Kingdom trades and cooperates more with European lands in a newer partnership, the **European Union.**

Unlike many countries, England still has a **monarch,** Queen Elizabeth II, who is also queen of the United Kingdom. The monarch lives in a palace, discusses government questions with the prime minister, and hosts government leaders from other lands. But the real government leader is the prime minister.

A Double-Decker Bus Drives In Front Of Modern-Day Parliament In London

©Robert Holmes/CORBIS

★London

The Royal Family Watching A Ceremony In London

From Left To Right, Prince Philip, Queen Elizabeth II, And Prince Charles

Two Policemen, Also Called "Bobbies," In London

★London
•Brighton

©Dave Bartruff/CORBIS

A few people in England, especially in the county of Cornwall, have mainly Celts as ancestors. But most people in England are English. The English have a mixed background. Their ancestors include the Celts, Romans, Angles, Saxons, Vikings, and Normans who arrived long ago.

Since the 1950s, a number of people from former British Empire colonies have moved to England. They include people from the West Indies, Guyana, India, Australia, and Africa. Among other people living in England are Southeast Asians, Chinese, Americans, and Europeans.

©Charles & Josette Lenars/CORBIS

A Merchant Selling Whistles At A London Carnival

A Woman At An Antique Automobile Rally In Brighton

©Adam Woolfitt/CORBIS

In England, most people live in cities or towns. For some, home is an apartment called a *flat*. But most people live in small two-story houses with little gardens. Houses are often built of brick, stone, or cement blocks. When city people go shopping, they often see beautiful old shops, banks, churches, museums, and other buildings—as well as newer ones.

A Thatched-Roof Cottage And Garden In The Country Near Rye

©WildCountry/CORBIS

©Ric Ergenbright/CORBIS

In the country, most people live in cottages or houses. These are often in small villages called *hamlets*.

Two-Story Houses In Lower Slaughter

©Martin Jones/CORBIS

• Leeds

Rye •   • Lower Slaughter

Children On A School Playground Near Farnham

Farnham

Padstow Christchurch

©John Heseltine/CORBIS

Schoolgirls On Their Way To An Exam In Christchurch

©Karan Kapoor/CORBIS

All English children between the ages of 5 and 16 must go to school. Most attend state schools paid for by the government. Children from wealthier families may attend "public" schools paid for by their families. (They are a bit like what we call "private" schools in the United States.) English "public" schools have more money for teachers, art supplies, and other things. Students at these schools usually live in big houses that are attached to the classrooms and other buildings.

England's official language is English. It is based on the German spoken by Angles and Saxons, and the French spoken by Normans long ago. But words from many other languages, including Celtic, Latin, and Norwegian, are also part of English. English has changed a lot over time, and it keeps on changing.

A Restaurant Sign In Padstow

THE PIG TROUGH

PADSTOW 520623

LICENSED RESTAURANT

©Johnathan Smith; Cordaly Photo Library Ltd./CORBIS

In the past, many English factories were powered by coal. Today many run on oil or natural gas from under the North Sea, or on nuclear power. English factory workers make such things as cars, airplanes, china teapots, woolen mittens, and computer software.

A Sheep Farmer On The Moors Of North York

©Patrick Ward/CORBIS

Many English people have service jobs. They serve their own people, as well as people from other lands, in hotels, tourist offices, banks, shops, museums, and insurance offices.

In the country, some English people farm, raising sheep, cattle, hogs, barley, vegetables wheat, and potatoes. Some mine coal, stone for building, or clay for making dishes. Others extract oil and natural gas from deep underground.

A Worker Assembling An Engine At The Rolls Royce Factory In Crewe

©Jerry Cooke/CORBIS

Crewe • Stoke-on-Trent

North York
Moors

©Annie Griffiths Bell/CORBIS

A Woman Painting Figurines At A Factory In Stoke-on-Trent

A Chef Cooking At A Japanese Restaurant In London

Norwich

★London

CORNWALL

©John Heseltine/CORBIS

Many English dishes use foods people can get easily. Lamb from English farms makes *Lancashire hot pot*, a lamb and vegetable stew. Milk from English cows makes cheeses such as Cheddar and Stilton. Seacoast fish and farm potatoes make fried fish and chips, a favorite takeout meal. In recent years, English farmers have started growing sugar beets. Their sweetness flavors English puddings such as *trifle*.

A Produce Stand At A Market In Norwich

©Michael S. Yamashita/CORBIS

People from other lands have also brought their foods to England. There are restaurants serving everything from American hamburgers to Italian pizza to Indian curries and Japanese sushi.

©Adam Woolfitt/CORBIS

A Miner Having A Tea Break In Cornwall

English people enjoy staying at home, gardening, fixing up the house, playing video games, reading, and watching TV. English TV shows are often so good that they find their way to other lands, including the United States.

Riding horses, bicycling, walking in the country, and bird-watching are other activities the English enjoy. Some people keep a lifelong list of all the different birds they've seen. Among favorite sports are cricket, soccer, rugby, lawn bowling, golf, and tennis.

English **bank holidays** are holidays when banks close. Bank holidays are Christmas and Boxing Day, New Year's, Good Friday and Easter Monday, May Day (the first Monday in May), Spring Bank Holiday (the last Monday in May), and Summer Bank Holiday (the last Monday in August). Special events often take place on bank holidays. One is the cheese race in the county of Gloucestershire. A huge round cheese is rolled down a hill and people chase it. Whoever catches the cheese gets to keep it.

The English have a special sense of fun. Maybe someday you'll visit their interesting country and join in it!

A Cricket Player In Cambridge

Liverpool

Cambridge

★ London

Cornwall Area

Rugby
Players In
Liverpool

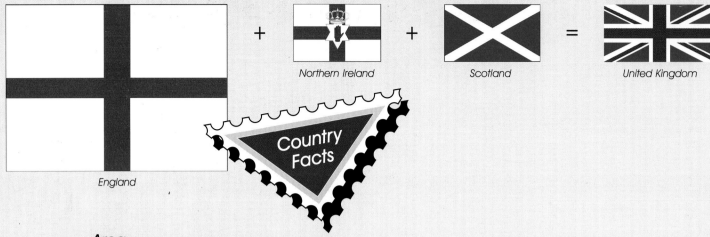

England + Northern Ireland + Scotland = United Kingdom

Area
About 50,000 square miles (130,000 square kilometers)—about the same size as Alabama.

Population
49 million people.

Capital City
London.

Other Important Cities
Birmingham, Leeds, Sheffield, and Liverpool.

Money
The pound sterling—also called a "pound." One pound is made up of 100 pence.

National Drink
Tea.

National Sports
Cricket in summer, soccer and rugby in winter.

National Flag
A red cross on a white square, called "The Cross of St. George." It stands for England's special saint. The flag for the whole United Kingdom (England, Scotland, Wales, and Northern Ireland) is called the "Union Jack." It is a combination of the flags of England, Scotland, and Northern Ireland.

National Song
"God Save the Queen."

Heads of Government
The prime minister of England is in charge of the government. The Queen of England works with the prime minister but does not have official powers.

A Royal Guard Protecting The Home Of The Queen's Mother In London

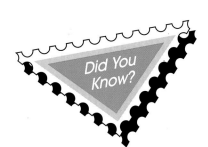

Did You Know?

Most English families have a pet, often a dog or cat.

*In 1620, the ship Mayflower took English **Pilgrims** across the Atlantic Ocean to what is now Massachusetts. The Pilgrims started Plymouth Colony, New England's first lasting European settlement.*

In 1994, the Channel Tunnel, or "Chunnel," opened under the English Channel. It has an underwater, underground railway that carries passengers between England and France.

An English pub is a social club, bar, and restaurant, all in one. Pubs serve sausages with mashed potatoes and other filling meals that don't cost too much.

English is one of the world's most widely spoken languages.

How Do You Say?

AMERICAN ENGLISH	BRITISH ENGLISH
apartment building	block of flats
elevator	lift
french fries	chips
garbage can	dust bin
phone booth	call box
sidewalk	pavement
sweater	jumper
truck	lorry

bank holidays (BANK HOL–ih–dayz)
Bank holidays are days in England when the banks close. Special events often take place on bank holidays.

British Empire (BRIH–tish EM–pire)
Colonies that belonged to England were part of the British Empire. England started these colonies during the reign of Queen Elizabeth.

colony (KOLL–uh–nee)
A colony is a country that is ruled by another country. England once had many colonies around the world.

continents (KON–tih–nents)
Most of the land areas on Earth are divided up into huge sections called continents. England is part of the continent of Europe.

European Union (yoor–uh–PEE–yun YOON–yun)
The European Union is a partnership among many of the countries of Europe. England is part of the European Union.

monarch (MON–ark)
A monarch is a person who rules over a kingdom. England's monarch is Queen Elizabeth II.

moors (MOORZ)
A moor is a huge area of open, grassy land. There are many moors in the southwest part of England.

Pilgrims (PILL–grims)
People who left England in the 1600s to live in the "New World" were called Pilgrims.

plateaus (pla–TOHZ)
Plateaus are flat areas that are higher than the lands around them. There are plateaus in some southwestern parts of England.

United Kingdom (yoo–NY–ted KING–dum)
The areas of England, Scotland, Wales, and Northern Ireland make up the United Kingdom.

Index

Web Sites

Learn more about England:
http://www.lonelyplanet.com/dest/eur/eng.htm

Learn more about the United Kingdom:
http://www.emulateme.com/unitedkingdom.htm

Take a virtual tour of the United Kingdom:
http://www.ontheline.org.uk/explore/journey/uk/ukindex.htm

Take a fun, musical tour of the Tower of London:
http://www.toweroflondontour.com/kids/index.html